10
STEPS CLOSER TO
GOD

"OVERCOMING BARRIERS THAT PREVENT REACHING YOUR FULL POTENTIAL IN GOD"

TAMMY SWAFFORD JONES

MULTIMEDIA COMPANY

10 STEPS CLOSER TO GOD
by Tammy Swafford Jones

Published by Majestic Multimedia Company
P.O. Box 570878   Orlando, FL 32857
info@majestic4us.com

This book or parts thereof may not be reproduced in any form, stored in a retrieval system, or transmitted in any form by any means – electronic, mechanical, photocopy, recording, or otherwise – without prior written permission of the publisher and/or author, except as provided by United States of America copyright law.

Unless otherwise noted, all Scripture quotations are from King James Version (KJV) used by permission of public domain.

Scripture quotations marked (NIV) are taken from the Holy Bible, New International Version ®. Copyright © 1973, 1978, 1984, 2011 by Biblica, Inc. ™ Used by permission of Zondervan. All rights reserved worldwide.

Intellectual Property of this content is secured under legal ownership and guardianship of Tammy Swafford Jones and/or authorized beneficiaries of estate as of publication date September 29, 2017 – and shall continue perpetually in the United States of America, continental territories and throughout the known universe.

Copyright © 2017 by Tammy Swafford Jones
All Rights Reserved

Edited by: Elaine J. Studer

ISBN-13: 978-0996533263
ISBN-10: 0996533265

Printed in the United States of America

*S*pecial thanks to the

Author and Finisher of my faith...

And they overcame him by the blood of the lamb and by the word of their testimony.
Rev. 12: 11

This book is a testimony of God's Greatness!

Dedication

This book is dedicated to
Terence (Terry) Andrew Swafford.

My life has not been the same since you have been gone.

Nevertheless, the precious memories of you will continue to live on.

Love,

Mom

Endorsements

To God be the Glory! I really enjoyed reading this book. It brings applicable biblical principles for all readers to apply in their everyday lives. It will inform and remind readers that unforgiveness is a sin! This book reinforces that the evil one, "Satan" comes to kill, steal, and destroy those of us who love God.

The benefit of this book is constant obedience to God and His words so that the overflow of blessings will follow. I like best about this book, at the introduction; when the author states how she came to God, and she will never turn back!

Rev. Rodney L. Eaton Sr.

Associate Minister Trinity Baptist Church

Richmond, VA

This book was very enlightening and informational. A new Christian would benefit greatly in their walk. If this book had been available to me when I was new in Christ, I would have avoided many spiritual tragedies. It was an easy read. I can't wait to see where God take you in your writing career. AWESOME BOOK!

Ms. Barbara Wright-Lucas

"10 Steps Closer To God", is a great resource tool for discipleship, for seekers, new and seasoned believers. It outlines the steps in easy layman's terms to understand how one can accomplish a closer walk with God in their lives. Each step helps one understand and reevaluate their position in achieving, maintaining and maturing their walk with God.

Tammy Swafford Jones' transparency, about her own struggles to have a closer walk with God, makes us realize that life is a journey, a work in progress. I highly recommend this book to anyone who desires to know what steps do I need to embrace to have a closeness to God on a daily basis.

Desiree Israel

Tammy Swafford Jones steps are ordered by God. This book is a must for new believers as well as mature believers, we all have fallen short of the glory of God. This book has the necessary basics to have a closer relationship with God and experience His presence as we remain consistent, applying these ten steps will get you where you need to go and keep you where you need to stay. All church organizations should have this book for their new converts class in training new members the bases in becoming a lifetime Christian.

Bridget T. McQuiller

Table of Contents

Introduction xi
Step 1: REPENT 1
Step 2: FORGIVE 13
Step 3: FAITH 21
Step 4: PRAYER 29
Step 5: DEVOTION 39
Step 6: STUDY 43
Step 7: BAPTISM & HOLY SPIRIT 47
Step 8: FASTING 57
Step 9: DISCIPLE 67
Step 10: OBEDIENCE & BLESSINGS 73
Thank you! 77
Abbreviations 79

NOTICE:

As a personal rule, I do not give advice on situations I have never experienced unless the Lord gives me words of knowledge to speak. For example, I could not give someone information on the divorce process because I have never been divorced.

Therefore, I would be giving my sole opinion, and if I'm wrong, my opinion could be more damaging than good. However, I do know firsthand about the breaking point in one's life. When we have that yearning desire to be closer to God, but sometimes lack the necessary steps to do so and lose hope.

Today, I am forever grateful to have an opportunity to share my personal experiences with you on the ups and downs of being a Christian.

Throughout my many downfalls and shortcomings, God has shown me through the Holy Spirit and His Word what He requires (His terms) to come closer to Him. As I took the initiative to follow God's order daily, a tremendous change began to take place in my spiritual well-being. I pray that these **10 Steps** *will strengthen, encourage, and usher you into a new place with God.*

INTRODUCTION

By the age of 15, my life had spiraled out of control. Most girls that age were preparing for cheerleader try-outs, but I was preparing for the arrival of my child. I felt lonely and hopeless, so I turned to the One I knew could help.

One Sunday afternoon during an altar call, a deep conviction came over me. It was a feeling that would not allow me to remain seated; as if something was nudging me to get up. Without hesitation I made my way to the front of the church with tears rolling down my face, I repented and dedicated my life to God.

I was uncertain why I felt such a divine peace at the altar, but I definitely wanted to remain in it. After my first altar call experience, I attended Sunday School, bible study, even choir rehearsal. I searched for answers on my level, answers that would give me in layman's terms "what to do next".

Five years had passed, and I felt my progress was minimal so I began church hopping (every Sunday a different church). I longed for anyone who was willing to take me under their arms and show me exactly what I needed to do. Eventually, I became frustrated because the Christian lifestyle seemed too difficult to achieve, so momentarily I gave up trying.

Unfortunately, I repeated that same cycle for many, many years, which always ended with the same discouraging results. Subconsciously I would fall back into my old sin, along with a few new ones. You see, the truth was I did not have a clue on how to maintain or mature as a Believer.

One evening after I put my children to bed, my mind began to ponder. At that moment I came to the conclusion that I could no longer fill this void in my life. I was spiritually dying and in dire need of help. I had longed for God throughout my childhood; and, as an adult, I still did not know how to grasp Him.

After hours of my mind wondering, I heard a low voice say, "Stop looking for answers in people and seek Me". That night I poured out to God, please show me they way. Since that night I learned to seek God foremost.

Since those days God has guided me to pastors that knew how to cultivate what God has placed in me. Today, I can truly proclaim that I am a devoted, never turning back Christian, operating in the gifts of prophecy, healing, and teaching; (gifts I did not know I had). Surprisingly, God is not finished working through me. He has done so many great things in my life that I never imagined could happen. **Hallelujah**!

Please stay encouraged, my friends, and always remember there is no respect (favoritism) of persons with God. He is the same yesterday, today, and forever!

He did it for me, and He will do the same for you!

Be blessed, with love,

Tammy Jaé

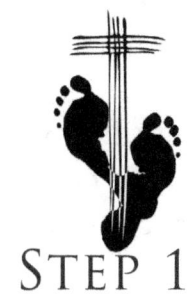

Step 1

Repent

R epent: To turn from sin and dedicate oneself to the amendment of one's life. b. To feel regret or contrition. c. To change one's mind. (WD)

Metanoeó (met-an-o-eh'-o) To think differently or afterwards, i.e. reconsider (morally, feel compunction): repent. Greek (SGL)

Each step in this book is vital; your progress is based on how accurately you follow each step. Change your mind and your actions will follow. God is calling all to repent!

And the times of this ignorance God winked at, but now commandeth all men every where to repent.
Acts 17:30 (KJV)
In the past God overlooked such ignorance, but now he commands all people everywhere to repent.
Acts 17:30 (NIV).

Therefore, just as sin entered the world through one man... **Romans 5:12 (NIV).**

Sin first entered into the world through God's first human creation. Everyone is born with a sinful nature, but that does not mean we should live a sinful lifestyle.

If we claim we have no sin, we are only fooling ourselves, and not living in the truth. **1 John 1:8 (NLT)**

Satan, sin, and deception go hand in hand, and the trio vindictively tries to find a way to enter into our lives. Satan's primary goal is to deceive us into believing we are not actually committing a sin. Adam and Eve were deceived the same way, they believed that a lie was the truth.

Please note that, that is a lie and a trick from the father of lies!
(emphasis John 8:44)

A thief comes to steal, kill, and destroy.
John 10:10 (KJV)

The thief (Satan) comes to *steal* our dreams, hope, joy, faith, peace, and ambition. He wants to *kill* our purpose and destiny by making us believe we are not who God says we are. Once the lie has taken its hold, the believer becomes discouraged and loses hope.

Therefore, allowing their destiny and purpose to be killed. For centuries his main tactic was and is to **destroy** our relationship with God by using the deception of sin.

MY TESTIMONY:

I can recall a period in my life when Satan deceived me. The words he spoke in my head, I believed. My motto was "Hurt them before they hurt me". I vengefully created a so-called "Dating Adventure" To-Do-List. I believed not a man on this earth was great enough to marry me.

In addition, I did not want to be limited to one man when I could change men like the weather. No, I did not believe I was committing a sin, I was not a cheater, fornicator, nor a liar. I thought I was merely being me. My heart was hardened against marriage (honestly, men too), just the mention of marriage made my stomach sick.

Satan had my eyes blinded, mind controlled and my actions were irrational to everyone except me. I was put in harm's way because of my reckless decisions and games which took me into a place of repentance. Once I drew closer to God, He broke me free from Satan's hold of deception. As my mind and heart changed God allowed me to see marriage in His perspective. "I is married now" **(Color Purple quote).**

God honors marriages and anything God honors, Satan dishonors and hates. ***Sin blocks prayers!***

Behold, the LORD's hand is not shortened, that it cannot save; neither his ear heavy that it cannot hear:

But your iniquities have separated between you and your God, and your sins have hid his face from you, that he will not hear. Isaiah 59:1-2 (KJV)

Surely the arm of the Lord is not too short to save, nor His ear too dull to hear. But your iniquities (sins) have separated you from God; your sins have hidden his face from you so that He will not hear. Isaiah 59:1-2 (NIV)

We know that God does not listen to sinners. He listens to the godly person who does his will. John 9:31(NIV)

We all have sinned and fallen short of God's glory, therefore, we all must confess. Any unconfessed sin will separate us from God, and He will not hear our prayers.

For the wages (price) of sin is death; but the gift of God is eternal life through Jesus Christ our Lord.
Romans 6:23(KJV)

Not only does sin hinder our prayers, but it will also result in eternal death/separation from God forever. **Sin has a stench!**

These are a smoke in my nose, a fire that burneth all the day. Isaiah 65:5 (KJV)

These people are like a stench in my nostrils an acrid smell that never goes away. Isaiah 65:5 (NLT)

Sin has a stench, an unpleasant smell to God's nostrils. The best way to describe a scent similar to sin is hot tar. Basically, when you and I sin (*lie, steal, gossip, fornicate, adultery, etc.*), we are literally applying this hot tar to our bodies. Afterward, we are left with the residue of that sin upon us, and that is the reason God turns His head away from sin. **Wouldn't you?**

Get ready; it is time to do some cleaning!

If we confess our sins, He is faithful and just to forgive us our sins, and to cleanse us from all unrighteousness.
1 John 1:9 (KJV)

God's desire is to cleanse us from the stench of sin. He is patiently awaiting your confessions. Yes, He knows all about every word, thought, secret, hidden agenda, lies, and deed that has ever occurred in our lives.

Even though, God knows all and sees all, He still requires everyone to confess all of their wrongs (sins) openly to Him whether we think they were justifiable or not. No sin we have committed is too big for God to forgive. *All* sins are equal because they all lead to separation from God. *(emphasis Romans 6:23) Therefore, you must stop doing the things that cause a separation from God!*

Micah 7:19, He will turn again,
He will have compassion upon us;
He will subdue our iniquities;
and thou wilt cast all their sins
into the depths of the sea. (KJV)
He will come back and comfort us again.
He will throw all our sins into the deep sea. (ERV)

Repent and turn to God, so that your sins may be wiped out, that times of refreshing may come from the Lord.
Acts: 3:19 (NIV)

It is **good news** to know that God does not hold our past against us (if we ask for forgiveness). We will be totally set free from the bondage and condemnation of sin. God is willing and able to forgive without judging.

The nature of the sin does not matter, whether it was: murder, rape, robbery, prostitution, adultery, abuse, incest, jealousy, abortion, hate, greed, lying, gossip, or stealing, just to name a few.

For all have sinned, and come short of the glory of God.
Romans 3:23 (KJV)

God wants to do a refreshing in your life!

I am going to use *"spring cleaning"* as an example, when spring arrives we begin to sweep, dust, and dig deep to throw away old things we no longer has a use for. After an extensive cleaning is completed, the house is now clean and refreshed; this is similar to how God wants His children cleaned. God wants our temples (bodies) cleansed and refreshed. It is time to repent and throw out your old ways of thinking and actions that are displeasing to God.

Now is the time to repent!

It is **imperative** that your prayer of repentance is sincere and honest or it will not be accepted by God. Find a quiet area in your home or any place where there will be

no interruptions, privacy is necessary because your conversation is between you and God.
Many times, I have been asked this question: *"Does God want us to be specific about our sins?"*
My answer is, **YES!**

I want to make this point very clear; God wants us to be specific about our known sins.

Whoever conceals his transgressions will not prosper, but he who confesses and forsakes them will obtain mercy.
Psalms 28:13 (ESV)
But then I decided to confess my sins to the LORD. I stopped hiding my guilt and told you about my sins. And you forgave them all! Selah.
Psalms 32:5 (ERV)

The 2*nd* Phase in *Step 1* is a Repentance Prayer; this is where, you confess your sins to God, turn away from the sin (stop doing it) and ask for forgiveness.

If we confess our sins, He is faithful and just and will forgive us our sins and purify us from all unrighteousness.
1 John 1:9 (NIV)

Prayer: Repentance

Heavenly Father, I have sinned in many ways. Your word declares if I confess my sins that You are faithful and just to forgive and cleanse me from all unrighteousness.

*Today, Lord I (**confess my sins**) and I ask for forgiveness, I repent (turn away) of every sin; I have committed against You, others, and myself. Father God, I ask for You to make my* *crooked path straight. I accept you into my life, heart, mind and soul as my Lord and Savior to cleanse and remake me into the person You have created me to be. Father, I accept the plans that You have for my life.*

Now, Father, I thank You for mercy, salvation, and forgiveness.

In the Name of Jesus,' I pray, Amen.

If you honestly and sincerely prayed the **Repentance Prayer**, your sins have been forgiven. **Yes!** It was just that easy. God does not make it difficult for us to come close to Him.

I must be honest, a few challenges will arise. Old sins will try to enter back into your life. However, with each step you complete in this book, you will learn how to maneuver around each obstacle and continue to move forward in God.

Don't give up!

Know ye not that they which run in a race run all, but one receiveth the prize? So run, that ye may obtain.
1 Corinthians 9:24 (KJV)
You know that in a race all the runners run, but only one runner gets the prize. So run like that. Run to win! **1 Corinthians 9:24 (ERV)**

Do not give up, because you are closer than you think. This Christian walk is all about pressing, pressing past what it looks and feels like, while keeping your focus on God.

For we walk by faith, not by sight...
2 Corinthians 5:7 (KJV)

REPENT DAILY
One of his disciples said unto him, Lord, teach us to pray, as John also taught his disciples.
And he said unto them, When ye pray, say, Our Father which art in heaven, Hallowed be thy name. Thy kingdom come. Thy will be done, as in heaven, so in earth.
Give us day by day our daily bread.
And forgive us our sins; for we also forgive every one that is indebted to us. And lead us not into temptation; but deliver us from evil.
Luke 11:1-4 (KJV)

Daily we must ask for forgiveness of sins we have committed throughout the day, sins of commission (known) and ommission (unknown). As God is cleansing you, hidden sin (unaware sin) will begin to surface, once you recognize it, repent.

Remember, repenting and asking for forgiveness should be a daily practice, especially during prayer. We have not reached perfection, yet. God is still doing a transformation in our lives, He is cleaning out the old to prepare us for the new. Amen! **Don't go back!**

Therefore if any man be in Christ, he is a new creature: old things are passed away; behold, all things are become new.
2 Corinthians 5:17(KJV).
Therefore, if anyone is in Christ, he is a new creation. The old has passed away; behold, the new has come.
2 Corinthians 5:17 (ERV)

STEP 1: REPENT

You are now a new person in Christ. Therefore, you cannot continue doing the old things you use to do (profanity, smoke, get drunk, etc.). Your new lifestyle must reflect Christ because YOU are a child of the Most High God!

For if we sin wilfully after that, we have received the knowledge of the truth, there remaineth no more sacrifice for sins. **Hebrews 10:26 (KJV)**
If we decide to continue sinning after we have learned the truth, then there is no other sacrifice that will take away sins. **Hebrews 10:26 (ERV)**

After we have learned the truth about God and still continue in sin, there are no other options. Jesus is the first and the last choice.

You must allow God to help you change because change does not come overnight, so do not get discouraged my friend, you are heading in the right direction. **Pray about it!**

Confess your faults one to another, and pray one for another, that ye may be healed. The effectual fervent prayer of a righteous man availeth much.
James 5:16 (KJV)
So always tell each other the wrong things you have done. Then pray for each other. Do this so that God can heal you. Anyone who lives the way God wants can pray, and great things will happen.
James 5:16 (ERV)

If you are continually committing the same sins, please pray and ask God to help you. Also, you can confess to someone you trust **(ie. *Pastor or fellow believer - This person must be Spirit-filled and have a God-led life*)** and allow them to pray and help you through it.
Resist sin.

1 Corinthian 10:13 says, *No temptation has overtaken you except what is common to mankind. And God is faithful; he will not let you be tempted beyond what you can bear. But when you are tempted, he will also provide a way out so that you can endure it.*
The ERV says, *The only temptations that you have are the same temptations that all people have. But you can trust God. He will not let you be tempted more than you can bear. But when you are tempted, God will also give you a way to escape that temptation. Then you will be able to endure it.*

You must keep in mind that sin and temptation will continually try to enter into our lives because sin is what Satan uses to keep us separated from God. Instead of falling into sin, make the perfect choice to resist it.

Resist the devil, and he will flee from you.
James 4:7 (KJV)

Congratulations, you have completed the first step!

STEP 1 : REPENT

Scriptures on Repentance

2 Chronicles 7:14
Proverbs 28:13
Matthew 4:17
Matthew 9:13
Luke 15:10
Acts 3:19
James 4:8
1 John 1:9
2 Peter 3:9

NOTES:

_____
_____
_____
_____
_____
_____
_____
_____
_____
_____
_____
_____
_____
_____
_____
_____

Please take notes and write down what God spoke to you or how each chapter has inspired you.

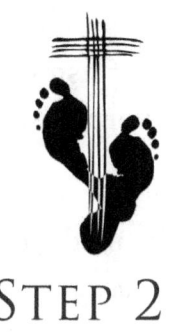

STEP 2

*F*ORGIVE

F orgive: To stop feeling angry or resentful toward someone who has done something wrong, to stop blaming someone (WD).
Apoluo (ap-ol-oo'-o): To free fully, i.e. (literally) relieve, release, dismiss, let die, depart, dismiss, divorce, forgive, let go, loose, send away, set at liberty. Greek (SGL)

Release the past and move forward in your future and in the promises of God.

- *Do you know unforgiveness blocks prayers?*

- *Do you know unforgiveness is a sin?*

As I stated in *Step 1,* any sin separates us from God and hinders our prayers.

A WEAPON OF MASS DESTRUCTION

Unforgiveness is similar to a weapon of mass destruction, but instead of using this powerful weapon of destruction against the perpetrator, you are actually using it against yourself.

Let me explain, in medical terms, *a foreign object is "something that is in the body but does not belong there"*. It can be inserted accidentally or intentionally. It also can become lodged or stuck in various parts of the body, and the 1# symptom is **pain!**

Unforgiveness is very similar to having a foreign object in your body, it is unseen, but you can definitely feel it. Unforgiveness can destroy you from the inside out.

Many factors can come into play with unforgiveness:
- *Unforgiveness can cause stress*
- *Unforgiveness can cause health issues*
- *Unforgiveness can cause isolation*
- *Unforgiveness can cause depression*
- *Unforgiveness can cause anger, hatred, and frustration*

UNFORGIVENESS PRODUCES

Unforgiveness also resembles the life of a plant. A plant has life because it has roots. If you nurture a plant, it will grow, but if you destroy the roots, it will die. Unforgiveness starts with one main root (foreign object), and it begins to grow.

If unforgiveness is ignored, and not dealt with quickly, it will produce *bitterness, resentment, hatred, along with a stony heart (hard heart).* An unforgiving heart is a **stony** heart in the eyes of God.

Ezekiel 36:26 (KJV) *A new heart also will I give you, and a new spirit will I put within you: and I will take away the stony heart out of your flesh, and I will give you a heart of flesh.*
Ezekiel 36:26 (NLT) *And I will give you a new heart, and I will put a new spirit in you. I will take out your stony, stubborn heart and give you a tender, responsive heart.*
Psalms 51:10 (KJV) – *Create in me a clean heart, O God; and renew a right spirit within me.*
Psalms 51:10 (NLT) *Create in me a clean heart, O God. Renew a loyal spirit within me.*

My friend, *all hope* is not lost. The more you choose to forgive (*it's a choice*) God will help you to remove that heart of stone. Once forgiveness has taken place that stubborn root of unforgiveness must decrease.

TIME TO FORGIVE

For if you forgive other people when they sin against you, your heavenly Father will also forgive you. But if you do not forgive others their sins, your Father will not forgive your sins. **Matthew 6:14-15 (NIV)**

Now, here is where the challenge awaits; God has forgiven you, now **you must** forgive others who have hurt, abused or misused you. Forgiveness is mandatory in order to move closer to God.

Forgiveness is like a two-way street; you cannot receive forgiveness from God if you are unwilling to forgive others. Yes, it may be a struggle, but God's desire is to release you from all those past hurts.

MY TESTIMONY

I am very familiar with unforgiveness. I also know forgiveness is easier said, than done. I dealt with unforgiveness for many years. I did not realize that I was carrying the heavy burden and not the person. The people who wounded me had moved on with their lives, while I was stuck in the past, depressed, oppressed and lonely.

Over the years, I allowed that root to build a thick wall of hatred, bitterness, and resentment around my heart. I hated the molester, rapist, abusive ex-boyfriend, and my son's murderer. My personal life was a wreck, as I tried to cover my pain with Hennessey.

My health declined as issues of high blood pressure, high cholesterol, and weight gain took its toll. I was restless, broken, hopeless, angry, and sometimes violent as the contemplation of murder or suicide crossed my mind. I was on the verge of losing my sanity. I was totally blind to the fact that unforgiveness was slowly destroying me. Listen, no one should have that much control over another person's life.

As God began to restore me, He revealed that those walls had to be broken, and the work had to come from within. I knew my ultimate goal and desire was to be closer to God. (I know your desire is the same because you are reading this book.) I did whatever it took to accomplish my goal and forgiveness was a mandatory start. You see, the bottom line was, God could not release me into my destiny until I let go of my past.

Leviticus 19:17-18 (ERV) says, *Don't secretly hate any of your neighbors. But tell them openly what they have done wrong so that you will not be as guilty of sin as they are. Forget about the wrong things people do to you. Don't try to get even.*
Romans 12:9 (ERV) *My friends, don't try to punish anyone who does wrong to you. Wait for God to punish them with His anger. In the scriptures, the Lord says, "I am the one who punishes; I will pay people back".*

AGAPE LOVE

God wants us to have an agape love (unconditional love) for each other. A love that has no boundaries, because it's the same love that God has for us. Do not allow peoples' actions to harden your heart and detour you away from this precious love.

For we wrestle not against flesh and blood, but against principalities, against powers, against the rulers of the darkness of this world, against spiritual wickedness in high places.
Ephesians 6:12 (KJV)
For we are not fighting against human beings but against the wicked spiritual forces in the heavenly world, the rulers, authorities, and cosmic powers of this dark age.
Ephesians 6:12 (GNT)

It's a Choice

I made a choice to forgive those that intentionally wounded me physically, emotionally, and mentally. As a result, the pain I had carried for almost 30 years was lifted. I did my part, and Our Gracious God did the rest. After all that lost time, I finally came to the understanding that my unfortunate circumstances were not my fault.

But I say unto you, Love your enemies, bless them that curse you, do good to them that hate you, and pray for them which despitefully use you, and persecute you. **Matthew 5:44 (KJV)**

Prayer: Unforgiveness

(I strongly encourage you to pray this prayer of forgiveness or a similar one in your choice of words.)

Lord, you have forgiven me, now I choose to forgive all those who have offended, abused, and misused me. ***(Mention each person by name and how they hurt you).***
Father, You said in ***Luke 4:18****, that You came to set the captives free. Lord, set me free from unforgiveness and take away all this hurt and pain. I am not strong enough to do this on my own Father; I need Your help, guidance, and strength.*
In the Name of Jesus of Nazareth, I pray, Amen.

*Remember forgiveness is similar to a two-way street (not a One way), forgiveness goes both ways.

Scriptures on Forgiveness

Ephesians 4:31-32
Matthew 6:12-1
Mark 11:25
Matthew 18:15-22
Luke 6
1 Peter 3:9
Colossians 3:1
James 5:16
Luke 17:3-4
1 John 1:9
Proverbs 15:1
Proverbs 15:18

NOTES

_____
_____
_____
_____
_____
_____
_____
_____
_____
_____
_____
_____

Congratulations, you are two steps closer to your goal!

STEP 2 : FORGIVE

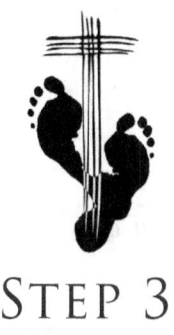

STEP 3

F aith 1. confidence or trust in a person or thing. 2. belief that is not based on proof. (D.C.)
Pistis (pis-`tis) faith, belief, trust, confidence, fidelity, faithfulness. Greek (S.C)

*As you take each step in this book, **faith** is required.*

Faith is the substance of things hoped for, the evidence of things not seen.
Hebrew 11:1 (KJV)
For we walk by faith and not by sight...
 2 Corinthians 5:7 (KJV)
If you can believe, all things are possible to him who believes...
Mark 9:23 (KJV)

I just love those verses, God wants us to truly believe in Him and to know that He can do anything but fail. Sometimes we cannot see God at work with the physical eye, but we must believe (by faith) that God is working on our behalf.

SNIPPET

As a child, I was raised in a Baptist church, but as an adult, I gravitated to many different denominations. I found myself solely depending on Pastor(s), denominations, and people to help me grow in Christ. (God does not want us to solely dependent on anyone, except Him.)

Eventually, I began to lose hope and faith, due to what I didn't see happening in my life. Over a period of time, I learned that no person could physically or spiritually take me higher in God. No other way could work except a personal relationship with Him. The more I began to spend time alone in His presence and Word, the more He instructed me. His way taught me how to live a fulfilling Christian life pleasing to Him and not people.

Do not get me wrong! *I still have days when I can't see a way out. The difference between then and now is, I do not lose my faith, I use my faith!*

For we walk by faith, not by sight...
2 Corinthians 5:7 (KJV)

Step out on faith!

Stepping out on faith reminds me of the woman with the issue of blood. For twelve years, she exhausted all her money on doctors that could find no cure. Now, when Jesus came on the scene, she believed (faith) that if she could just touch the hem of His clothes; she would be healed; and, true indeed, she was healed.

Jesus said, *"Your faith has made you whole (healed)."* (Paraphrased) *Mark 5:21-34*

You see, her faith alone was not enough, but she used her faith by touching His clothes. Faith requires works. Faith is not just sitting and waiting for something to happen; faith is ***getting up, stepping out and allowing God to step in.***

Faith is an action word!

My brothers and sisters if a person claims to have faith but does nothing, that faith is worth nothing. Faith like that cannot save anyone. Actions must accompany your faith. Faith without any actions is dead faith. Actions are what brings your faith to life.

What is FAITH?
- *Faith is believing God.*
- *Faith is turning your thoughts and words into action.*
- *Faith is seeing past the impossibilities.*
- *Faith + actions = POWERFUL RESULTS!*
- *Faith is believing God will work all things out for your good.*
- *Faith is the opposite of doubt.*
- *Faith has no boundaries, restrictions or limits.*
- *Faith is taking the limits off of God.*

- *Faith is knowing that you serve a God who can do anything but fail.*
- *Faith gives God glory.*
- *Faith is believing and receiving the Promises of God.*

He staggered not at the promise of God through unbelief; but was strong in faith, giving glory to God.
Romans 4:20 (KJV)

My Testimony

In 2004, I arrived early to my first sonogram appointment. I was overwhelmed with anticipation to know the gender of my baby. As the technician applied the warm gel and scanned my belly, she revealed, "It's a boy!" After my ultrasound, I was directed to go inside a conference room where the OB-Gyn doctor met me.

Once I was seated, the Doctor began asking basic questions pertaining to the family tree. After I had given him all the information I knew, he continued to ramble on about Multicystic dysplastic kidney.

Finally, he spoke my language with words a mother never wants to hear. "The fetus is not developing." He continued on saying, "The fetus has one functional right kidney and several cysts surrounding the left kidney". I kept my composure as my emotions went in every direction possible. After a short pause, he recommended an abortion due to my child having a very slim chance of surviving.

To make a long story short, I chose not to abort; and, through prayer and faith, I gave birth to a healthy baby boy, despite his illness. He was not a sickly baby; however, he did *require periodic ultrasounds and renal scans to monitor the kidney function and growth of cysts. My son was 5 yrs. old when the Urologist detected that the cystic kidney had dissolved without a trace.*

*Today, my son's one miracle kidney is functioning like two, and I am grateful to say, "He is living a normal life!" When the Doctor said "**No!**" God overruled and said "**Yes!**"*
Hallelujah, Glory be to God!

DOUBT IS THE OPPOSITE OF FAITH!

Without faith, you will always be doubting yourself and displeasing God, but with faith, you are pleasing God, trusting in Him, and believing that it can be done. As believers in Christ, we must have faith.

Without faith, it is impossible to please God because anyone who comes to Him must believe that He exists and that He rewards those who earnestly seek Him.
Hebrew 11:6 (NIV)
Because you have so little faith. Truly I tell you, if you have faith as small as a mustard seed, you can say to this mountain "Move from here to there," and it will move. Nothing will be impossible for you.
Matthew 17:20 (NIV)
So Jesus answered and said to them, "Have faith in God." "For assuredly, I say to you, whoever says to this mountain, Be removed and be cast into the sea and does not doubt in his heart, but believes that those things he says shall come to pass; he shall have whatever he saith. "Therefore I say unto you, whatsoever things ye desire,

believe that you receive them, and ye shall have them."
Mark 11:22-24 (KJV)

The mountain in the above scripture symbolizes obstacles and situations in our lives. These are circumstances that cannot be moved under normal conditions, but with a **little faith,** nothing is impossible. **God specializes in the impossible!**

How to increase your faith

- The Bible states that God has given each one of us a measure of faith. **(Romans 12:3)**
- Pray for an increase in your faith.
- Read the Bible. Faith comes by hearing, and hearing by the Word of God. **(Romans 10:17)**
- Take chances with God. Your Faith will increase the more you use it.

Prayer for Faith

Heavenly Father, I boldly come before Your throne of grace. Today, I anchor my trust in you. Father, Your Holy Word says, whatsoever I bind on earth shall be bound in heaven and whatsoever I loose on earth shall be loosed in heaven. Right now, I bind every thought of negativity and doubt, and I release hope and faith in my life. I now know that having faith pleases you and I am a God pleaser.

In Jesus Mighty Name, I pray, Amen.

Scriptures on Faith

James 1:3
1 John 5
James 1
1 Peter 1:7-9
James 5:14
1 Corinthians 13:2
Mark 10:52
Romans 1:17
Matthew 9:28-29
Romans 10:10

NOTES

Step 4

Prayer

P rayer: to speak to God especially in order to give thanks or to ask for something. (WD)
Proseuchomai (pros-yoo'-khom-ahee): I pray, pray for, offer prayer. Greek (SC)

Prayer is simply talking to God

Prayer is a highly important step; I cannot stress enough how vital this step must continually be in your life daily. Prayer is the highest form of worship, it is simply communication from you to God, through spoken words, thoughts, songs, letters, poems, and meditation.

The Lord is near to all who call on him, to all who call on him in truth;... **Psalms 145:18 (NIV)**

Sincere prayers from the heart develop a personal relationship with God. Without prayer as a daily part of your life, the relationship between you and God will not flourish. You cannot have friends or be in a relationship without some form of communication.

I must communicate with my husband, children, family, and friends regularly to keep our relationships afloat. This basic requirement applies both in the physical realm with family and friends and in the spiritual realm with God. Prayer is the *lifeline* that keeps us connected to God.

We must pray!

We are not exempt from prayer, Jesus, the holiest man that ever walked this earth prayed. Below are a few passages of Jesus praying and His prayers:

And in the morning, rising up a great while before day, he went out, and departed into a solitary place, and there prayed.
Mark 1:35 (KJV)

Our Father which art in heaven, Hallowed be thy name. Thy kingdom come, Thy will be done in earth, as it is in heaven. Give us this day our daily bread. And forgive us our debts, as we forgive our debtors. And lead us not into temptation, but deliver us from evil: For thine is the kingdom and the power, and the glory, forever. Amen.
Matthew 6: 9-13 (KJV)

At that time Jesus answered and said, I thank thee, O Father, Lord of heaven and earth, because thou hast hid these things from the wise and prudent, and hast revealed them unto babes.
Matthew 11:25-26 (KJV)

And when he had sent the multitudes away, he went up into a mountain apart to pray...
Matthew 14:23 (KJV)

He went out into a mountain to pray and continued all night in prayer to God.
Luke 6:12 (KJV)

And being in an agony, he prayed more earnestly: and his sweat was as it were great drops of blood falling down to the ground.
Luke 22: 41-44 (KJV)

Jesus lifted up his eyes, and said, Father, I thank thee that thou hast heard me. And I knew that thou hearest me always: but because of the people which stand by I said it, that they may believe that thou hast sent me.
John 11:41-42 (KJV)

Now is my soul troubled; and what shall I say? Father, save me from this hour: but for this cause came I unto this hour. Father, glorify thy name. Then came there a voice from heaven, saying, I have both glorified it, and will glorify it again.
John 12:27-28 (KJV)

Pray through Worship

So, through Jesus, we should never stop offering our sacrifice to God. That sacrifice is our praise, coming from lips that speak his name; Hebrew 13:15(ESV).

The Bible tells us that the angels say, "*Holy, holy, holy, Lord God Almighty*" **(Rev. 4:8).** Yes, even the angels worship God, and we **must** worship and adore Him too.

The Bible tells us that if we keep quiet and do not praise Him, the rocks will immediately cry out. **(Luke 19:40)**

> ...I definitely do not want any rocks praising my God for me!"

Reasons to pray

- *Prayer increases our spiritual and physical strength. (Isaiah 40:29)*
- *A prayerful lifestyle will keep the heaven above you open. (Deuteronomy 28:23), (Luke 3:21)*
- *Prayer invites God's will into our lives. (Jeremiah 29:12-13)*
- *Prayer gives us peace. (Isaiah 26:3)*
- *Prayer gives us hope. (Romans 12:12)*
- *Prayer increases our faith. (Matthew 7:7-11)*
- *God hears our prayers. (1 John 5:14)*
- *God delights in our prayers. (Proverbs 15:8)*

There are no limits, restrictions, boundaries, or excuses as to why we are not able to pray. God loves you; and He wants **you** to spend some quality time with Him.

I love those who love me, and those who seek me find me; **Proverbs 8:17 (NIV)**

Side Note: God is not a genie in a bottle, He should not be a once a week…pray when we need something, God. God is not to be used for His blessings but adored for His Greatness!

WHAT'S NEXT?

Now, that we've covered why we should pray, I want to discuss the *how, what, when and where* to pray.

When: *Begin with setting aside some personal time out of your busy schedule to talk with God. Set a daily schedule that works best for you, morning, afternoon, evening, or all three.*

- *David said evening, morning, and at noon will I pray and cry aloud, and He will hear my voice.* **(Psalms 55:17)**
- *Seven times a day do I praise thee because of thy righteous judgments.* **(Psalms 119:164)**
- *Jesus prayed in the early morning* **(Mark 1:35)** *and throughout the night.* **(Luke 6:12)**

Where: *The Bible states, when we pray to enter into a secret place.* Praying in private keep our prayers from being vain. God does not want to hear a performance, only sincerity gets His attention.

But when you pray, go into your room, close the door and pray to your Father (God) who is unseen. Then your

STEP 4 : PRAYER

Father, who sees what is done in secret, will reward you openly. Matthew 6:6 (NIV)

You can also pray while on your lunch break, driving, cooking, cleaning, or otherwise.

How: Positions have different significance. They shows the expression of our prayers. If feasible you should try different postures. However, the position is not nearly as important as the prayer itself.

Below is a list of posture positions:
- Kneel - keeps us humble, a surrender to God's authority. **(1 Kings 8:54, Ezra 9:5, Psalms 95:6)**
- Bow – shows respect to God, gratitude, and worship. **(Exodus 34:8)**
- Stand - a willingness to serve, shows honor. **(Nehemiah 9:5)**
- Walk - **(2 Kings 4:35)**
- Sit – shows weariness. **(Nehemiah 1:4)**
- The lifting of hands – shows worship, surrendering, glory to God. **(1 Timothy 2:8)**
- Lay prostrate- (lying face down on the floor) shows total submission to God, humility. **(Genesis 17: 3)**

Please keep in mind that you are entering into the presence of the King of all kings, Lord of all lords, and The God of all gods. A Sovereign, Almighty, All Majestic, All Righteous God, so position yourself accordingly.

*Side Note: God gave me instructions several years ago to wash and anoint my face, hands, and feet and cover my head with my prayer shawl. Since then there has been a tremendous shift in my prayers.

*What: The Bible says to **pray without ceasing**.*
*(**1 Thessalonians 5:17**), which simply means keep God in your mind and heart at all times.* **I've learned that "Thank you, Jesus" is a simple prayer, I say it throughout the course of the day.**

Lastly, there is a multitude of issues that requires our prayers: family members, our cities, illnesses, confession, forgiveness, thankfulness, missing children, marriages, depression, homelessness, suicide, violence, and the list goes on.

Many people are in need of prayer, so we as believers must intercede (*pray*) on behalf of others. There is strength in numbers, so it is always good to pray with other Christians.

Again, I tell you that if two of you on earth agree about anything you ask for, it will be done for you by my Father in heaven. For where two or three gather in my name, there am I with them.
Matthew 18:19-20 (NIV).

Note: I've only addressed the basics and importance of prayer. There are different levels of prayer and as God increases in your life, so will your level of prayer.

Prayer: Teach me how to pray

Holy One, Anointed One, My Sovereign God. Father, I thank You, for the Grace to seek You through prayer. I humbly ask that you teach me how to pray in a way that is pleasing to You.

Teach me how to spend time in prayer and intercede for others, teach me how to boldly speak prayers that will break bonds and destroy yokes. Heavenly Father, teach me Your perfect will and Your perfect way.

In Jesus Mighty Name, I pray Amen.

You are on the right path, keep moving forward!

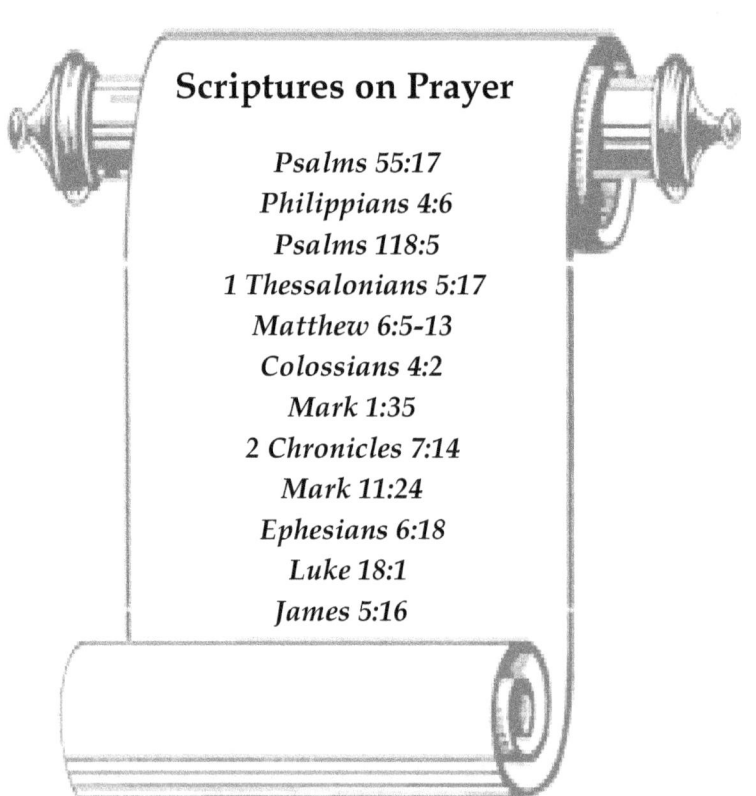

Scriptures on Prayer

Psalms 55:17
Philippians 4:6
Psalms 118:5
1 Thessalonians 5:17
Matthew 6:5-13
Colossians 4:2
Mark 1:35
2 Chronicles 7:14
Mark 11:24
Ephesians 6:18
Luke 18:1
James 5:16

Notes

STEP 4 : PRAYER

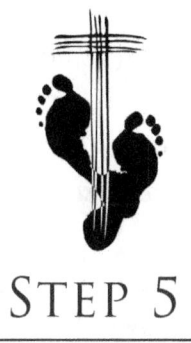

STEP 5

D evotion(s): A feeling of strong love or loyalty, the quality of being devoted. Prayer, worship, or other religious activities that are done in private rather than in a religious service. (MW)

Proskartere`o (pros-kar-ter-eh`-o): To persist, preserve in, to continue to do something with intense effort. With the possible implication of despite difficulty. To devote oneself to. Greek (SC)

For the eyes of the LORD range throughout the earth to strengthen those whose hearts are fully committed to him.   2 Chronicles 16:9 (NIV)

So far, you have repented, forgiven, and are exercising your faith. You are definitely on the right track with your relationship with God.

STEP 5 : DEVOTION

Now is the moment to devote **yourself** and your **time**. Devotion is simply dedication, and it consists of setting aside time daily to give **God Glory**, **Honor**, **Praise**, and to acknowledge *Him* as your *Lord.*

Worthy are you, our Lord and God, to receive glory and honor and power.   Revelation 4:11 (ESV)

Devotion goes beyond a weekly church service. Corporate devotion is greatly needed in our lives, but God wants some one on one time with **You**.

One day is simply not enough, devotion should be done on a daily basis. Believe me, I know how easy it is to get distracted by what's going on around us, family, job, social media... and lose focus on God.

The devil's plot is to keep our focus on what's happening around us, *which leads to* spending little to no time with God. Whatever our circumstances, we must make time for *God (no excuses).*

<u>10 Devotion Tips</u>
1. *Put God first!*
2. *Begin with a minimum of 15 minutes per day.*
3. *If you do not spend quality time with God, you can not receive the fullness of God.*
4. *Daily devotion must become a habit, a lifestyle.*
5. *If you want others to see the Light of God through your life, you must spend time in His presence. We must be an example.*

6. *You must be consistent in your quality time with God.*
7. *Devotion consists of reading a scripture (preferably Psalms and/or Proverbs), prayer, sitting in silence and meditating on God, or musical worship.*
8. *Record your thoughts and what you hear from God in a journal. Also, you can record answers to prayer in your journal.*
9. *Everyone's quiet time with God varies, allow your heart to guide you into a personal, unique devotion.*
10. *Devotion helps us from falling back into our old ways (sins).*

DEVOTION PRAYER

Heavenly Father, forgive me for not always putting you first. Lord, I am a work in progress, so I thank you for Your patience with me. I thank You for the privilege of being able to come into your presence to sit and spend time with You; quality time that should not be taken for granted. Father God, I give you permission to instruct and teach me Your Perfect Way.

In Jesus Name, I pray, Amen.

Devotion Scriptures

Psalms 1:2
Psalms 46:10
Psalms 62:1
Psalms 119:9
Matthew 6:33

STEP 5 : DEVOTION

Notes

STEP 6
STUDY

S tudy: The commitment of time and attention to acquiring knowledge on an academic subject, especially by means of books.
Meletao` (mel-et-ah`-o): To devise, plan, practice, exercise myself in, study, and ponder. (SC)

As a Christian, it is mandatory to study the Word of God. You **must** read the bible and know what the word of God says for yourself and not from the mouths of others (grandma, mother, pastor, etc.).

2 Timothy 2:15 (KJV) *states, "Study to shew thyself approved unto God, a workman that needed not to be ashamed, rightly dividing the word of truth."*

Do your best to present yourself to God as one approved, a worker who does not need to be ashamed and who correctly handles the word of truth. (NIV)

Growth in God is good and necessary. Do not get comfortable with where you are in God because there is so much more to experience. Take your limits off!

Reasons to Study:

- *We prove our devotion to God by studying His Word.* **2 Timothy 2:15**
- *Studying increases our knowledge of God.* **John 17:3, 2 Peter 3:18**
- *Studying increases our wisdom in God.* **Colossians 1: 9-10, 3:16**
- *Studying increases our faith.* **Romans 10:17, James 1:22-24**
- *The Word of God is an instruction manual for our lives.* **2 Timothy 3:16-17**
- *The Word of God is our spiritual food.* **1 Timothy 4:6, 1 Peter 2:2**
- *God speaks to us through scriptures.* **Proverbs 6:22**
- *To be fully equipped and ready for any questions someone may ask.* **1 Peter 3:15**
- *The Word of God directs us.* **Psalms 119:105**
- *The Word of God is QUICK and POWERFUL!* **Hebrews 4:12**
- *The Word of God is an offensive and defensive weapon for Christians.* **Ephesian 6:19**

As you are studying, memorize and meditate on God's Word, **do not rush** through it, allow yourself some study time *(start with at least 15-30 minutes per day).*

Keep this Book of the Law always on your lips; meditate on it day and night, so that you may be careful to do everything written in it. Then you will be prosperous and successful. **Joshua 1:8 (NIV)**

Blessed is the one who does not walk in the counsel of the wicked or stand in the way of sinners or sit in the seat of mockers. But whose delight is in the law of the Lord, and who <u>meditates</u> on his law day and night. That person is like a tree planted by streams of water, which yields its fruit in season and whose leaf does not wither. Whatever they do prospers. **Psalms 1:1-3 (NIV)**

Studying can be done alone or with a Bible-based study group that can help you grow deeper in God's Word.

As newborn babies, desire the sincere milk of the word, that ye may grow thereby. **1 Peter 2:2 (KJV)**

Like newborn babies, thirst for the pure milk of the word so that by it, you may grow in your salvation.
1 Peter 2:2 (ISV)

There are many study guides, educational, devotional, and inspirational books that can help you gain a greater spiritual insight. Amazon is a great place to shop for reasonably priced books.

Prayer: Studying God's Word

Father, I thank you, because You said in Your Word, "If I ask I shall receive." Today, I ask that you will take me deeper and unlock my understanding. Teach me how to study, grant me wisdom, knowledge, and understanding of Your Holy Word. Lord, I choose to study and show myself approved unto You and rightly divide Your Word of truth.

In Jesus' Name, I pray. Amen

Study Scriptures

Joshua 1:8
Job 23:1
Psalm 119:1
Romans 10:17
2 Timothy 3 16-17
Hebrew 4:12

Notes

_____
_____
_____
_____
_____
_____
_____

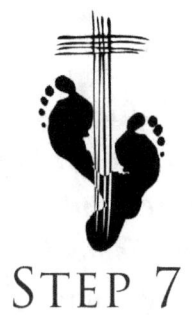

STEP 7

Baptism & Holy Spirit

B aptism: A Christian ceremony in which a small amount of water is placed on a person's head or in which a person's body is briefly placed under water. (WD)
Baptizo: dip, submerge, but specifically a ceremonial dipping. (Greek) (SC)

God wants our lives to be in order according to His will and not ours. In *Step 7*, I have combined the subjects of *The Holy Spirit* and *Baptism* together because they are similar to a hand in a glove, they fit together perfectly.

Repent, and be baptized every one of you in the name of Jesus Christ for the remission (forgiveness) of sins, and you shall receive the gift of the Holy Ghost...
Acts 2:38 (KJV)

Over the past few years, I have met several people who felt the Holy Spirit or baptism was not necessary. Well, I am here to tell you that is another lie from the father of lies, Satan!

BAPTISM

Did you forget that all of us became part of Christ Jesus when we were baptized? In our baptism, we shared in his death. So when we were baptized, we were buried with Christ and took part in his death. And just as Christ was raised from death by the wonderful power of the Father, so we can now live a new life. **Romans 6:3-4 (NIV)**

Baptism symbolizes the burial of our old sins and deeds. Our former lifestyles are buried, and now we can start a fresh new lifestyle with Christ. Baptism is also a public declaration of your confession and belief in Christ.

Baptism is not secondary; it is necessary!

Now, don't wait any longer. Get up, be baptized and wash away your sins, trusting in Jesus to save you.
Acts 22:16 (ERV)
He that believeth and is baptized shall be saved; but he that believeth not shall be damned. **Mark 16:16 (KJV)**

We need God's gift of the Holy Spirit just like we must have water. You and I can not walk this path alone, we need the assistance and guidance of the Holy Spirit.

The Holy Spirt helps us maintain a Christ-like lifestyle. The Holy Spirit teaches us the truth and gives us an understanding of who God really is. The Holy Spirit also brings conviction, correction, and stability into our lives.

Let us look at what the scriptures say; *"Verily, Verily, I say unto thee, except a man be born of water (baptism) and of Spirit (Holy Spirit), he cannot see the kingdom of God.* **John 3:5 (KJV)** As you see, the Holy Spirit is not optional, but <u>mandatory</u>.

<u>The DNA of Christ</u>

Now if any man have not the Spirit of Christ, he is none of His. Roman 8:9 (KJV)
But whoever does not have the Spirit of Christ does not belong to Christ. (ERV)

Naturally speaking, at the time of conception, a baby receives 100 percent of each of its parents' DNA. The child's DNA verifies who the biological parents are.

Spiritually speaking, when a sinner is reborn through baptism, we receive the DNA of Christ, which is the gift of the Holy Spirit.

<u>How do I receive the Holy Spirit?</u>
- The Bible tells us that the Holy Spirit is a gift. **(Acts 2:38)**
- Pray and ask God for the Holy Spirit. **(Luke 11:13)**
- I strongly encourage you to seek a Biblical-based Pastor or Leader to further instruct you with more insight into the Holy Spirit.

MY TESTIMONY

I was baptized when I was 12 years old. I was unsure what baptism meant, but in those days you did what you were told with no questions asked. Following my baptism, I stayed on my knees for hours (repeatedly saying "Thank you Jesus") trying to receive the Holy Spirit.

I became discouraged because nothing happened. Discouragement allowed me to believe that the Holy Spirit was not for everybody, especially me.

*At the age of 22, while I was washing dishes something odd happened. I heard a low voice say "**John 3:5**." Immediately I stopped and grabbed the Bible to read the scripture. After I read the verse, I became disappointed once again, until I realized how God truly loved me. He wanted me to know that without the Baptism and His Spirit I could not enter into His Kingdom, so once again I fell to my knees; and nothing happened.*

As a child, I often saw my mother on her knees speaking in an unfamiliar language (tongues). I was quite familiar with the language of the Holy Spirit, but I did not know how to receive it. By my early thirties, I still had not received the Holy Spirit.

*I searched the scriptures for answers and **Luke 11:13** caught my attention "**Ask Him.**" At that very moment, I prayed and asked God for the gift of the Holy Spirit. A few weeks later, I was baptized a second time with an understanding.*

After my second baptism, I devoted myself to a daily worship and prayer regimen in my secret place. One afternoon, while in worship something came over me; I had no control of my language (I spoke with other tongues), and I could actually feel the presence of God. My memory is vague as to how long it lasted, however, it was an experience I will never forget.

Spiritually Food for Thought!

The Lord knoweth them that are His. (2 Timothy 2:19)

I want you to visualize standing over a colony of ants and marking some of the ants with bright white dots. Despite the thousands of ants in that colony, you will be able to quickly pinpoint the ones with the white dots.

Because they are different than the rest. This is the same scenario with God; It does not matter how many billions of people are on this earth. God can look down on us and quickly pinpoint His children by the Light of His Holy Spirit that shines so bright.

Prayer: The Gift of the Holy Spirit

Heavenly Father, I thank You for allowing me to know You in a deeper way.

Father, You said in Your Holy Word, "Ask and it shall be given."

Father, I humbly come asking for the gift of the Holy Spirit to endow, guide, instruct, and equip me for what You have for my life.

Father, I thank and praise you in advance for the gift of the Holy Spirit.

In Jesus' Name, Amen.

During the course of this Christian walk, we can feel spiritually drained and disconnected from God. Don't worry, my friend, the Holy Spirit has not left you!

Yes, we can grieve the Holy Spirit **(Ephesians 4:30)** by falling back into sin. However, the Holy Spirit is a gift from God, and He does not take it back.
(Ephesians 1:13-14, John 14:16)

During this time of spiritual depression, we must remain focused and stand on the *Promises of God*. Here are a few of His *Promises*:

My covenant will I not break, nor alter the thing that is gone out of my lips. **Psalms 89:34 (KJV)**
No, I will not break my covenant; I will not take back a single word I said. (NLT)

For all the promises of God in him are yea, and in him Amen, unto the glory of God by us.
2 Corinthians 1:20 (KJV)
For all God's promises are "Yes" in him. And so through him, we can say "Amen," to the glory of God. (ISV)

And the LORD, he it is that doth go before thee; he will be with thee, he will not fail thee, neither forsake thee: fear not, neither be dismayed. **Deuteronomy 31:8 (KJV)**
The LORD himself goes before you and will be with you; he will never leave you nor forsake you. Do not be afraid; do not be discouraged. (NIV)

The Lord shall fight for you, and ye shall hold your peace.
Exodus 14:14 (KJV)
The Lord will fight for you; you need only to be still. (NIV)

He giveth power to the faint; and to them that have no might he increaseth strength. **Isaiah 40:29 (KJV)**
He gives strength to the weary and increases the power of the weak. (NIV)

But they that wait upon the LORD *shall renew their strength; they shall mount up with wings as eagles; they shall run, and not be weary and they shall walk, and not faint.* **Isaiah 40:31 (KJV)**
But those who trust in the LORD will find new strength. They will soar high on wings like eagles. They will run and not grow weary. They will walk and not faint. (NLT)

Fear thou not; for I am with thee: be not dismayed; for I am thy God: I will strengthen thee; yea, I will help thee; yea, I will uphold thee with the right hand of my righteousness. **Isaiah 41:10 (KJV)**
So do not fear, for I am with you; do not be dismayed, for I am your God. I will strengthen you and help you; I will uphold you with my righteous right hand. (NIV)

For I have satiated the weary soul, and I have replenished every sorrowful soul. **Jeremiah 31:25 (KJV)**
I will refresh the weary and satisfy the faint. (NIV)

The righteous cry and the LORD *heareth, and delivereth them out of all their troubles.*
Psalms 34:17 (KJV)
The LORD hears his people when they call to him for help. He rescues them from all their troubles. **(NLT)**

Therefore I say unto you, What things soever ye desire, when ye pray, believe that ye receive them, and ye shall have them.   **Mark 11:24 (KJV)**
Therefore I tell you, whatever you ask for in prayer, believe that you have received it, and it will be yours. **(NIV)**

And we know that all things work together for good to them that love God, to them who are the called according to his purpose.
Romans 8:28 (KJV)
And we know that God causes everything to work together for the good of those who love God and are called according to his purpose for them.   **(NLT)**

We must remain strengthened with the **Word of God** because the enemy desires to sift us like wheat (*Luke 22:31*). *Christians do fall down, but we don't stay down!*

Sometimes we have to be like David and encourage ourselves, but today, I encourage you to get up and put on the *Full Armour of God* **(Ephesians 10-18).**

Someone's salvation is depending on **you**!

Prayer: Refreshing of the Holy Spirit

Father, I enter into Your gates with thanksgiving and Your courts with praise.

I thank You for the gift of the Holy Spirit, Abba, I come asking for a refreshing of the Holy Spirit.

Refresh me, Renew me, Reinvigorate me Oh God; give me a burning zeal to serve and accomplish everything You have planned for my life.

In Jesus' Name, I pray, Amen.

Scriptures to Study

Baptism	/	Holy Spirit
Peter 3:21		John 3:8
Acts 2:38-41		John 14:26
Acts 16: 31-33		Acts 2:1-5
Acts 22:16		Acts 2:17
Luke 3:16		Corinthians 6:19
Luke 3:21-22		1 Corinthians 2:14
Mark 16:16		
Ephesians 5:18		

Notes

Step 8

Fasting

Fasting: abstain from all or some kinds of food or drink, especially as a religious observance. (D.com)
Tsum (tsoom): to abstain from food. Hebrew (SC)

Throughout the years, I have learned that *fasting* is very significant to our spiritual and natural well-being, yet we often neglect *to fast as we should*. Fasting spiritually disciplines our flesh (our natural body) because our flesh has had too much control in our lives, for too long.

The flesh constantly urges us to do things that are against the will of God like adultery, stealing, lying, gossip, laziness, overeating, jealousy, and envy, just to name a small few. At the same time, our Spirit wants to do the opposite of the flesh and only those things that are pleasing to God.

The flesh and spirit are in constant battle against each other!

So I tell you, live the way the Spirit leads you. Then you will not do the evil things your sinful self wants. The sinful self wants what is against the Spirit and the Spirit wants what is against the sinful self. They are always fighting against each other so that you don't do what you really want to do. **Galatians 5:16-17(ERV)**

THE POWER IN FASTING

The Bible gives us explicit details and end-results of great men and women who fasted. Below, I have listed a few people from the Bible who fasted for different reasons. It is surely amazing and encouraging to know how fasting and prayer have rewards beyond measure.

- **Moses-** *fasted for 40 days and 40 night afterwards he received the Ten Commandments.* **(Deuteronomy 9:9-11)**
- **Daniel-** *after a 21 day fast God blessed Daniel with wisdom beyond that of anyone else in the empire.* **(Daniel 10:1-3)**
- **Esther-** *Haman called for the annihilation of all Jews. Esther called for a three-day fast for all the Jews in her city. The result- the Jews were spared, and Haman was hanged on the gallows he built.* **(Ester 4:16)**
- **Hannah-** *could not bear a child. She "wept and did not eat". God heard her plea, and the prophet Samuel was born.* **(1 Samuel 1:7)**

- ***Ezra*** *- fasted for a safe journey for him, the children, and their possessions.* **(Ezra 8:21)**
- ***Saul*** *- God called him on the road to Damascus and shared the assignment for his life during the time when he neither ate nor drank and prayed.* **(Acts 9:7-9)**
- ***Jehoshaphat*** *- needed to know the Lord's plan to defeat an Army. Through a fast, God's plan was revealed and the Army was defeated.* **(2 Chronicles 20:3)**
- ***Elijah*** *- the word Elijah received during his fast affected even the next generation.* **(1 Kings 19:8)**
- ***Joseph*** *- fasted in prison. When released he became fabulously wealthy and was put over all the money of Egypt.* **(Gen. 41:39-45)**
- ***Solomon*** *- humbled himself in fasting and prayer and God greatly increased his wealth and wisdom* **(Kings 3:10-13)**
- ***Jesus*** *fasted for 40 days and 40 nights, which prepared Him to stand-up against the temptations of the tempter. Afterward Jesus; began His ministry of preaching the Gospel.* **(Matthew 4:1-17)**

BENEFITS OF FASTING

Fasting produces several great benefits; here are a few key points to keep in mind:

- *Fasting empowers our prayers. (Fasting gives our prayers an extra boost).*
- *There is Power in fasting! (Howbeit this kind goeth not out but by prayer and fasting. Mark 9:29 KJV)*

STEP 8 : FASTING

- *The desires of the flesh decrease when you fast.*
- *Fasting breaks strongholds*
- *Fasting + prayer = results*
- *Fasting is giving up something in the natural to get an enlightenment in the spiritual.*
- *There is spiritual growth in fasting.*
- *God moves miraculously during fasting.*
- *Satan hates when we fast and pray, and this is a reason to fast even more*

You must pray during your fast. (Fasting without prayer, is simply just not eating).

1. *Fast for a specific time and reason. (Set a start, end date, and tell God the reason for your fast.) Search for scriptures that relate to your fast, meditate on them and pray them aloud.*
2. *Fast on behalf of a loved one, personal issues, illness, etc.*
3. *Corporate Fast (Fasting along with others, church members, or under the leadership of your Pastor).*

Fasting is not as complicated as it may seem; however, a commitment is definitely required because distractions will try to come your way. You must commit to a fast and **do not allow** anything or anyone to throw you off course from your fast.

And when you fast, do not look gloomy like the hypocrites, for they disfigure their faces that their fasting may be seen by others. Truly, I say to you, they have

received their reward. But when you fast, anoint your head and wash your face, that your fasting may not be seen by others but by your Father who is in secret. And your Father who sees in secret will reward you.
Matthew 6:16-18(ESV)

That scripture speaks clearly that **when** we fast, do not go around telling everyone you are fasting; your fast is between you and God only. Fasting requires self-control and self-discipline while seeking the heart of God. Fasting is setting aside things that we normally enjoy like food.

Below is a list of Biblical Fasting examples:
- *Full fast (3 days, no food or liquids)*
    - *Esther's Fast – (Esther 4:16)*
    - *Saul's Fast – (Acts 9:9)*
- *Partial fast (fruits and vegetables) (Daniel 10:2-3)*
- *Beginners fast (12 am –noon, no food)*
- *Weekly fast (choose 1-2 days per week to turn down your plate *skip a meal*)*

Limit the use of the following items: cell phones, television, video games, the internet, and social media. By doing so, your attention can be directed towards God without distractions and when He speaks, you will clearly hear.

Start small and work your way up (*by that I mean, do not begin a 40 day fast if you have never fasted before unless you have been instructed by God to do so, fasting takes time*).

If you are taking medications or have a chronic illness, please be mindful and seek your Physician's advice on what best works for you.

FASTING BREAKS CHAINS

Is not this the fast that I choose: to loose the bonds of wickedness, to undo the straps of the yoke, to let the oppressed go free, and to break every yoke?
Isaiah 58:3-7(ESV)

Fasting can break the chains of addiction, fornication, drugs, pornography, overeating, etc.

MY TESTIMONY

A year had passed after I completely committed my life to God. I was on track until I fell back into the temptation of sin (fornication). I allowed my past desires to reopen a door and at that very moment, I sought to please myself instead of God. Many nights, God did not allow me to rest in my sin, but restless nights were not enough for me to give him up.

Instead, I tried to justify my sin by believing we were going to get married. (Later, I found out he was already married.) You see, the devil had me caught in his trap, again. Months later, I began to lose some interest in the married man (yes, I said some interest) because he could not fully commit, so Satan quickly sent a replacement to keep me bound in fornication.

One day while shopping I saw a lady I previously knew, and she gave me a prophetic word "The man you're dating is going to your husband." Despite my good news, every day a part of me felt like my life was in shackles as I prayed less and sinned more.

Until one night I had a disturbing dream of two naked men with Rams heads holding me down by my ankles and wrists, and the more I scrambled to break free the tighter their grip became. The following morning, I knew without a doubt God had revealed my life to me in a dream.

With tears in my eyes, I couldn't believe how naïve I had been, I believed a false prohet's words and I was caught up in Satan's trick . I had enough of being used, and I was ready to restore my relationship with God. Yes, I was emotionally attached, but I had to tell them that our relationship had come to an end.

A few weeks had passed, and I had not received a phone call from either man, but Satan was not finished trying. Late one evening I received a phone call from the married man explaining how he wanted to start over and move in together. It was extremely difficult because my heart wanted to say, "No, " but my flesh said, "Yes."

After I hung up the phone, I felt the urgency to pray, so I fell to my knees and cried out "God, please help me and remove anyone that's not meant to be in my life". That evening was the last time I spoke with him.

For months, I felt disgrace and guilt for turning my back on God to chase my desires. I was embarrassed beyond words to talk about what I had been doing in secret. Feelings of condemnation and confusion crept in, but somehow the scripture, **Confess your faults to another and pray one for another, that ye may be healed. (James 5:16 KJV)** *began to replay over and over in my mind.*

I was in desperate need of prayer, so I called and confided in a fellow sister in Christ. I expected her to pray, but instead, she shocked me with her response. She said, "You have to fast for two weeks." I was okay with fasting until she suggested eliminating the one thing I desired the most, a triple, triple coffee (3 creams and 3 sugars) from my favorite coffee shop. I responded, "Really!" I never imagined going a day without my coffee.

I did not quite understand what fasting from coffee had to do with fornication, but I agreed. The next day I started a fast; and I must admit it was a struggle. I was irritated, frustrated, and often tempted to get a cup of coffee, but I stood firm to the end. The last day of my fast, I anxiously waited in the coffee shop parking lot until the fast ended at 3:00. By 3:01, I was in line to purchase a cup, I ordered it just the way I loved it, and to my surprise, it tasted horrible.

My assumption was I received a bad batch of coffee beans. The following day I tried another triple, triple, but it tasted worse than the day before; and that is when I realized that during my fast God had freed me from my addiction to coffee and the stronghold of fornication.

Yes, I know coffee may seem minor, but it was not the coffee, it was my addiction to the coffee. Any addiction will have a bondage on our lives, and God does not want our lives bound, but free.

If the Son sets you free, you will be free indeed.
(John 8:36 NIV)

"Now, therefore," says the Lord, "Turn to Me with all your heart, with fasting weeping and with mourning" (Joel 2:12 NIV)

Prayer: Fasting

Heavenly Father, I thank you for Your Truth and Understanding. I thank You for being patient with me as I transition into being whom You have called me to be.

Father, I ask for further instructions on how to fast, a fast that is not vain but pleasing to You and beneficial for me. Father God, give me the strength, encouragement, and will power to fast and overcome every bound area in my life.

Father, I thank you.

In Jesus' Holy Name I pray, Amen.

Scriptures on Fasting

Joel 2:12
Psalms 69:10
Matthew 6:16-18
1 Corinthians 7:5
Isaiah 58:3-7.
2 Corinthians 3:6
John 3:8
Luke 18:1-12
1 Corinthians 2:14

Notes

Step 9

DISCIPLE

D isciple: One who accepts and assists in spreading the doctrines of another. (MW)
Math`et`es (math-ay-tes): A learner, disciple, pupil. Greek (S.C.)

Congratulations! You have completed *Steps 1-8*, and I truly believe that God is pleased as you are growing in Truth, Grace, and Knowledge of Him. As Christians, we are all called to be Disciples of Christ. Now, it is your duty as a disciple of Christ to share what you have learned of Our Savior.

What you have heard me teach publicly you should teach to others. Share these teachings with people you can trust. Then they will be able to teach others these same things. **2 Timothy 2:2 (ERV)**

As disciples we cannot be selfish, we must share our knowledge of God with others.

As iron sharpens iron, so one person sharpens another. **Proverbs 27:17 (ERV)**

We must do our part by continuing to spread the love & gospel of Christ like a wildfire throughout the earth.

We should think about each other to see how we can encourage each other to show love and do good works. We must not quit meeting together, as some are doing. No, we need to keep on encouraging each other. This becomes more and more important as you see the Day getting closer. **Hebrews 10:24-25 (ERV)**

YOUR GIFT WILL MAKE ROOM FOR YOU
(Proverb 18:16)

God has called each of us to work in his vineyard. We all have special gifts that are meant to be used to help others while bringing God glory. Basically what I am saying is, God gets the glory out of our gifts.

Everyone is not called into the five-fold ministry of apostles, prophets, evangelists, pastors, and teachers. However, your gifts and abilities are unique and important to the Body of Christ. Someone at this very moment needs to see and hear you, disciple.

The Body of Christ needs you, do not allow your gifts to lay dormant any longer. Now, is the time for you to go forth in your purpose and destiny!

God has given us the power and authority to call a thing forth. Today, my friend, I am calling forth the gift in you!

COME FORTH, PEOPLE OF GOD!

Come forth, Father!   Come forth, Mother!
Come forth, My Brother!   Come forth, My Sister!
Come forth, Writer! Someone needs to read your books.
Come forth, Poet! Someone needs to read your poems of affirmation.
Come forth, Speaker! Someone needs to hear your words of knowledge.
Come forth, Musician! Your music can break strongholds.
Come forth, Psalmist! Your voice can shift the atmosphere.
Come forth, Intercessor! Intercede on someone's behalf.
Come forth, Artist! Paint pictures for His Glory.
Come forth, Phone Ministry! Someone needs words of encouragement.
Come forth, Social Media Ministry! Spread the gospel around the world.
Come forth, Hospital Ministry! The sick need to be healed.
Come forth, Jail Ministry! Minister to the incarcerated.

My Testimony

When I started my duties as a disciple, I simply began with inviting people I met to my church and encouraging my family members. As God began to grow me in that area, I found my passion in outreach.

One day, the Lord showed me a vision of an outreach in a park that was considered a Red Zone area (addictions, poverty, etc.) in my city. My desire was to help people get free from bondage, so God used my testimonies as a beacon of hope. I joined along with a few others and began to bring the vision to fruition.

In first event we prayed, fed and clothed one hundred people and children. During our second annual event meet we the needs of more than five hundred people with prayer, food, and clothing, and **Praise God,** *we are still going strong.*

I encourage you, my sisters and brothers in Christ to stay firm in the Lord and continue to say, "YES," and allow Him to use you to encourage someone else.

**Faithful is He that called you, who also will do it.
(1 Thessalonians 5:24 NIV)**

Purpose and Destiny Prayer

Lord, I thank you for bringing me this far. Even when I felt like giving up, You helped me to hold on. Heavenly Father, I thank you for my purpose and destiny. Lord, I want to be a beacon in someone's life, as my life reflects Yours. Lord, I desire to be a willing vessel to promote your Kingdom here on earth. In Jesus name, Amen.

And Jesus came and said to them, "All authority in heaven and on earth has been given to me. Go therefore and make disciples of all nations, baptizing them in the name of the Father and of the son and of the Holy Spirit, teaching them to observe all that I have commanded you. And behold, I am with you always, to the end of the age." **(Matthew 28:18-20) (ESV)**

Discipleship Scriptures

1 John 1:9
John 8:31
John 13:34-35
Matthew 5:14-16
Luke 6:40
Luke 14:27
Luke 17:3-4
Luke 6:37
Proverbs 15:1
Ephesians 4:31-32
Colossians 3:13

Notes

STEP 10

OBEDIENCE & BLESSINGS

O bedience: compliance with an order, request, or law or submission to another authority.
Hupakoé (hoop-ak-o-ay'): obedience, submissiveness, compliance. Greek
Blessings: 1. the act or words of a person who blesses.
2. A special favor, mercy, or benefit.
Eulogia: (yoo-log-ee'-ah): adulation, praise, blessing, gift.

For a brief moment, all I could write was, **Wow**! I am proud of you, and you should be proud of yourself too! I know it was a bumpy road as you challenged yourself to keep moving forward, this book was only a stepping stone to get you past the barriers. Now you are limitless.

Please remember to maintain a lifestyle of *REPENTANCE, FORGIVENESS, FAITH, PRAYER, DEVOTION, STUDYING, FASTING, and SHOWING THE LOVE OF OUR FATHER TO OTHERS.*

GOD IS AMAZING!

When God told me to write this book, I heard the Lord say, "Blessings." Then He spoke, "Blessings come with obedience." So I began to search His Word on obedience and blessings.

*¹ And it shall come to pass, if thou shalt hearken diligently unto the voice of the L*ORD *thy God, to observe and to do all his commandments which I command thee this day, that the L*ORD *thy God will set thee on high above all nations of the earth:*

*² And all these blessings shall come on thee, and overtake thee, if thou shalt hearken unto the voice of the L*ORD *thy God.*

³ Blessed shalt thou be in the city, and blessed shalt thou be in the field.

⁴ Blessed shall be the fruit of thy body, and the fruit of thy ground, and the fruit of thy cattle, the increase of thy kine, and the flocks of thy sheep.

⁵ Blessed shall be thy basket and thy store.

⁶ Blessed shalt thou be when thou comest in, and blessed shalt thou be when thou goest out.

*⁷ The L*ORD *shall cause thine enemies that rise up against thee to be smitten before thy face: they shall come out against thee one way, and flee before thee seven ways.*

*⁸ The L*ORD *shall command the blessing upon thee in thy storehouses, and in all that thou settest thine hand unto; and he shall bless thee in the land which the L*ORD *thy God giveth thee.*

⁹ The LORD shall establish thee an holy people unto himself, as he hath sworn unto thee, if thou shalt keep the commandments of the LORD thy God, and walk in his ways.

¹⁰ And all people of the earth shall see that thou art called by the name of the LORD; and they shall be afraid of thee.

¹¹ And the LORD shall make thee plenteous in goods, in the fruit of thy body, and in the fruit of thy cattle, and in the fruit of thy ground, in the land which the LORD sware unto thy fathers to give thee.

¹² The LORD shall open unto thee his good treasure, the heaven to give the rain unto thy land in his season, and to bless all the work of thine hand: and thou shalt lend unto many nations, and thou shalt not borrow.

¹³ And the LORD shall make thee the head, and not the tail; and thou shalt be above only, and thou shalt not be beneath; if that thou hearken unto the commandments of the LORD thy God, which I command thee this day, to observe and to do them. **Deuteronomy 28: 1- 13 (KJV)**

Obedience to God's way brings forth blessings. Yes, we may experience some short comings, but God still gives us unmerited favor. We can buy material things, but we cannot purchase favor, this is a gift only from God. I encourage you to stay in right standing with God and receive the Blessing of **The Almighty God!**

So shalt thou find favour and good understanding in the sight of God and man. **Proverbs 3:4 (KJV)**

PRAYER

Father God, You are my Healer, my Redeemer, and my Keeper. You kept me when I did not know how to keep myself. You saved me and brought me out of the miry clay and set my feet upon a solid rock. Oh Lord, I thank you for provision, I thank you for favor. I thank you for when I wanted to quit and You spoke, "Finish!"

I thank you, for every reader of this book.

Jehovah Jireh, I speak Deuteronomy 28 1-14 over and in their lives, in the Name of Jesus! Lord of All, I pray that You will bless, instruct, and equip Your people with what they need to continue in Your Perfect Way.

In Jesus Name, I pray, Amen!

NOTES

*T*HANK YOU!

I want to say thank you, you all do not know how much I appreciate each and every one of you.

My father, Eric, I love you!

My mother, Birdida who guided me to God's path, but it is a road I must walk alone.

My husband, Alton. God exceeded my expectations when he blessed me with you.

My children, Terry, Terrell, ReShone (Jazmyn), Antoine (stepson), Jalisa (stepdaughter), Micah, Curtis, Akeem (stepson), Curvon, Torron, and Tristan. You gave me a new meaning to life. You all are my motivation, inspiration, and my blessings.

My grandchildren, Jaides (step), Jayden, JaTereon, Kyadine (step), Kodi (step), Imoni (step) and Cartier (step). You are the batteries, which keep my clock ticking.

My sisters, Pam (Mike), Angie (Quan), Toya, and Shonda (Mike). Love you to life!
My brother, Ernie. Love you!

My nieces and nephews, Auntie Tammy loves you!

My fathers, mothers, brothers, and sisters in Christ, bless you!

A special BLESS YOU to my beautiful sister, Bridgette M.

My sons and daughters in Christ. Jalisa (Chris), Tiffani, and Lawrence. I love you!

A special I love you, to my mentees, Barbara, Sada, Sharon, Uri, JoeAnn, Kenishasa, and Slyvestor.

Thank you Darselle for our newly formed blessed sisterhood. Your declarations give me joy!

Thank you, District Elder Pastor E. Kimberly Brown and Deacon Tony Brown. I thank you for your correction, love, support, and for stretching me beyond my reach. **"Love is what Love does."**

Thank you, Supt. Vincent Mathews Sr. and Mother Cheryl Mathews for teaching me how to stand on a foundation that can never be broken.

Thank you, Pastor Gary Rogan for your wisdom, kindness, and helping me to flourish.

Thank you, Carole!

Thank you, Periscope followers you are a portion of my strength.

Thank you, family and friends and everyone names I did not mention. I love you, all!

Abbreviations

- King James Version (KJV)
- New Living Translation (NLT)
- New International Version (NIV)
- English Standard Version (ESV)
- Easy to Read Version (ERV)
- Good News Translation (GNT)
- International Standard Version (ISV)
- Dictionary.com (DC)
- Webster Dictionary (WD)
- Strong's Concordance (SC)
- Strong's Greek Lexicon (SGL)
- Merriam-Webster (MW)

CONITUNUED NOTES

www.ingramcontent.com/pod-product-compliance
Lightning Source LLC
LaVergne TN
LVHW051509070426
835507LV00022B/3003